UNSOLVED MYSTERIES

BIGFOOT

BY JAMIE KALLIO

ABOUT THE AUTHOR

Jamie Kallio is a youth services librarian in the south suburbs of Chicago. She is also the author of several nonfiction books for children. Once she thought Bigfoot was in her backyard, but it may just have been her husband.

The Child's World®

Published by The Child's World®
1980 Lookout Drive • Mankato, MN 56003-1705
800-599-READ • www.childsworld.com

ACKNOWLEDGMENTS
The Child's World®: Mary Berendes, Publishing Director
Red Line Editorial: Editorial direction
The Design Lab: Design
Amnet: Production

DESIGN ELEMENT: Shutterstock Images

PHOTOGRAPHS ©: iStockphoto, cover; Kevin Lings/Shutterstock Images, 5; Laszlo Dobos/Shutterstock Images, 7; Tony Rowell/Corbis, 8; Steffen Foerster/Shutterstock Images, 11; Bill Schaefer/The Idaho State Journal/AP Images, 12, 23; Antonino Barbagallo/Corbis, 14; Emin Kuliyev/Shutterstock Images, 15; Nick Hewetson/Thinkstock, 19; Rene Drouyer/Hemera/Thinkstock, 20

ISBN 9781634070713
LCCN 2014959757

Printed in the United States of America
Mankato, MN
July, 2015
PA02266

TABLE OF CONTENTS

CHAPTER ONE

GIANT HAIRY BEASTS

In 1924, Fred Beck was searching for gold. Beck and four friends set up camp close to Mount St. Helens in Washington. They had often looked for gold nearby. The men had seen large footprints in the area. They thought mountain gorillas had made the prints. These gorillas were part of the local **folklore**. There were many reported sightings of them.

One night, the friends woke to a loud sound. Something was banging on their cabin wall. The men saw three giant hairy beasts outside. The

beasts walked on two feet like humans. They threw large rocks at the cabin. Two beasts climbed onto the roof. They jumped up and down. When the sun rose, the beasts ran off. The event frightened Beck and his friends. They left their camp the next morning.

Beck told others what he had seen. Many concluded that the beasts were mountain gorillas. They nicknamed the area

Ape Canyon. Some people had another idea. The beasts acted differently from most gorillas. They looked different, too. What if Beck had seen something else? Over time, researchers considered another possibility. Maybe he had seen Bigfoot.

What Is Bigfoot?

According to **legend**, Bigfoot is a giant hairy creature. It lives in forests or mountains. Like humans, Bigfoot is **bipedal**. People claim it has large feet. They describe its face and hands as looking very human.

Some campers say they have seen Bigfoot. Hikers and hunters also report Bigfoot sightings. They say that Bigfoot is often alone. Descriptions of the creature vary. According to reports, it stands 5 to 10 feet (1.5 to 3 m) tall. It is covered in black or reddish-brown hair. Some people say it smells bad. Most Bigfoot sightings happen at night. The creature may be

Many Bigfoot sightings have happened in forests.

nocturnal. However, people have also reported seeing it in the daytime.

People often talk about Bigfoot as if it is only one creature. But witnesses have reported Bigfoot sightings in many places and times. These witnesses may be seeing different creatures of the same **species**. Some people, like Fred Beck, have reported seeing more than one creature at a time. A few have reported family groups of creatures that look like Bigfoot.

History of a Legend

Bigfoot sightings usually happen in North America. Most occur in northwestern Canada and the United States. Native American tribes have told stories of Bigfoot for generations. But people have seen Bigfoot all over the world. The creature has different names in different places. In the southern United States, it is called Skunk Ape. Canadians call it Sasquatch, while Tibetans call it the Yeti. In Australia, people call it Yowie. Despite

This statue in northern California shows Bigfoot.

the different names, the descriptions of this creature are similar.

People have long told stories about giant, ape-like people. They started using the word *Bigfoot* in about 1958. In that year, a construction crew was building a road in northern California. One morning, the crew found that something had scattered their tools. It looked like a large creature had thrown a spare tire across the worksite. The tire weighed 700 pounds (318 kg). What creature could have thrown it?

The crew looked for evidence. They found giant footprints near a bulldozer. Then they told others what had happened. Newspapers reported on the mysterious creature with giant feet. They called it Bigfoot.

Soon, more people shared their Bigfoot stories. Some said they had seen the creature. Others had only seen its large footprints. The legend of Bigfoot was here to stay.

CHAPTER TWO

UNCOVERING BIGFOOT

Since 1958, researchers have looked for Bigfoot. They talk to witnesses and study large footprints. Yet many scientists do not believe Bigfoot exists.

The people who study Bigfoot are called cryptozoologists. They study **cryptids**, or creatures from legends. Scientists do not recognize these creatures as existing species. They are often **skeptical** of cryptids.

Bigfoot is one of the most famous cryptids. Another example is the Loch Ness Monster in Scotland. Some scientists think all evidence of

People once thought that the okapi was a myth.

these creatures is fake. But sometimes cryptids turn out to be real. The gorilla was once thought to be a myth. So was the okapi, a giraffe-like animal. Later, scientists discovered that gorillas and okapis were real.

Since the 1990s, hundreds of new animal species have been discovered. Scientists think that other unknown species exist. Could Bigfoot be one of them?

Bigfoot Evidence

Many people have reported finding large, strange footprints. Usually, they find these prints deep in the wilderness. Today, these footprints are the best evidence of Bigfoot. Sometimes hikers find one or two footprints in mud. Other times, they see long tracks of the large footprints. Researchers make plaster casts of the prints. They compare casts to find similar

A museum displays casts taken from possible Bigfoot footprints.

prints. Then they decide which prints are likely from Bigfoot.

Many scientists believe that if Bigfoot truly existed, there would be more evidence. No Bigfoot skeletons have ever been found. Photos and videos of the creature are often blurry. Some people also wonder why hunters have never caught Bigfoot.

Bigfoot researchers admit that evidence is hard to find. Whole animal skeletons are rare. Once a big animal dies, other animals carry most of it away. They scatter the bones. The creatures may also bury their dead in secret places. Some hunters say they have seen Bigfoot. Yet they did not want to catch the creature. They said it looked too human.

MYTH OR FACT?
People have reported thousands of Bigfoot sightings.

This is a fact. Several groups track Bigfoot sightings. One online database includes 30,000 reports. Experts think some reports are more believable than others. But most Bigfoot sightings are similar. Witnesses usually agree that Bigfoot is large, hairy, and bipedal.

Some people once thought that this photograph showed Bigfoot.

Until more proof is found, most scientists will not consider Bigfoot real. Researchers are still looking for evidence. Someday, they hope to convince the scientists. Perhaps then scientists can discover what Bigfoot really is.

MYTH OR FACT?

Researchers have discovered Bigfoot hair.

This is a myth. Many people have claimed that they found Bigfoot hair. In 2014, researchers sent samples to a scientist. The scientist studied more than 30 hair samples. Most were actually from cows or horses. Some hair was from a new species of bear.

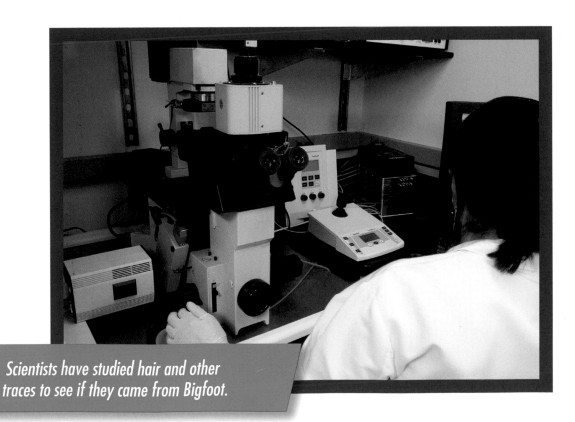

Scientists have studied hair and other traces to see if they came from Bigfoot.

CHAPTER THREE

THE SEARCH CONTINUES

Researchers face many challenges in finding Bigfoot. One challenge is from phony evidence. Many people have faked sightings of Bigfoot. Some want to become famous or make money. Others fake Bigfoot sightings as a joke. If Bigfoot is real, these tricks take time away from true efforts to find the creature.

Several people have made Bigfoot prints as a **hoax**. Ray Wallace made wooden carvings of big feet. He used these carvings to create "Bigfoot prints" all over California. Others have faked films of hairy, human-like creatures. In 2010, John Rael made a video of an ape-like beast. The creature was running through a forest in Oregon. Later, Rael explained that the video was not real. He created it to show how easily evidence could be faked. The "beast" was a man in a costume.

MYTH OR FACT?
Edmund Hillary had the scalp of a Yeti.

This is a myth. Bigfoot is called the Yeti in parts of Asia. In 1960, explorer Edmund Hillary traveled to a mountain range in Asia. Villagers gave him what they said was a Yeti scalp. Scientists tested the object. It was actually the skin of a serow. A serow is an animal similar to a goat.

Researchers disagree on whether some evidence is fake. In 1967, a rancher made a film. It shows a hairy, human-like figure. The rancher said this figure was a female Bigfoot. The creature looked real. Twelve scientists studied the film. Some decided it was a hoax. Others could not tell if it was real or a very good fake. Even today, some experts are not sure.

Hoaxes are not the only problem for Bigfoot researchers. Many sightings turn out to be mistakes. People only think they see Bigfoot. They might really see prints from other large animals, or from humans. Or they may glimpse bears running through the forest. Researchers say most Bigfoot sightings are mistakes.

Bigfoot Theories

If Bigfoot does exist, what is it? Researchers have some **theories**. Bigfoot could be a type of ape. A giant ape called *Gigantopithecus* once lived in Asia. Evidence of the ape is from thousands of years ago. It is thought to have gone extinct. But perhaps some apes survived. They could have traveled to North America. Another theory is that Bigfoot is a surviving **Neanderthal**. Some early humans were Neanderthals. They were heavier than humans today. They had sloping foreheads and wide faces. Modern humans developed more than 150,000 years ago. Then Neanderthals died out. But small groups of them may have remained.

A third theory is that Bigfoot is an orangutan. Orangutans have orange or reddish-brown hair. Most live alone. They hide in forests. This could explain why Bigfoot

This illustration shows an artist's idea of what a Neanderthal looked like.

sightings are rare. In southern Sumatra, Bigfoot is called the Orange Pendek.

Protecting Bigfoot

Why do researchers want to find Bigfoot? Partly, they want to know what the creature is. It could be a new species. Many people are interested in Bigfoot because it is human-like. Studying the creature could help scientists understand people better.

Some researchers also want to protect the creature. They think Bigfoot is dying out. Reports of sightings have

Many orangutans live alone in forests.

gone down over time. Some people think that Bigfoot's numbers are declining. The creature's **habitats** may have been destroyed. Perhaps its food sources have become scarce. By finding Bigfoot, researchers could learn how to help. They could provide food and shelter for the creature. Researchers fear that without this help, Bigfoot might not survive.

Many groups are searching for Bigfoot. One is the Bigfoot Field Researchers Organization. This group has members with different jobs. Some are cryptozoologists. Some are scientists. They all want to uncover the mystery of Bigfoot.

These groups work hard, but many believe it is not enough. They want governments to help. Governments could provide special equipment. They could also train teams of scientists. These teams could find evidence more easily.

A big search might finally uncover Bigfoot. Until then, no one has proof that this creature exists. People who believe in the legend will continue searching. One day, we may discover the truth.

Glossary

bipedal (BYE-peh-dal) A bipedal animal walks on two feet. Researchers say that Bigfoot is a bipedal creature.

cryptids (KRIP-tidz) Cryptids are animals whose existence is not proven by science. Bigfoot and the Loch Ness Monster are cryptids because there is no clear proof that they exist.

folklore (FOHK-lor) The stories and beliefs people pass from generation to generation are a culture's folklore. Bigfoot is a part of the folklore of many Native American tribes.

habitats (HA-bih-tats) Habitats are animals' homes. Some people want to help Bigfoot by protecting its habitats.

hoax (HOHKS) A hoax is a trick or joke. Some people created large footprints as a hoax to convince people that Bigfoot existed.

legend (LEJ-und) A legend is a traditional story that is not necessarily true. Many cultures have a legend of a hairy, two-legged beast in the wilderness.

Neanderthal (nee-AN-der-tawl) A Neanderthal is a type of early human. Some people think Bigfoot is a surviving Neanderthal.

nocturnal (nok-TUR-nuhl) A nocturnal animal sleeps during the day and is awake at night. Bigfoot may be nocturnal, because most people see the creature at night.

skeptical (SKEP-ti-kul) When people are skeptical, they doubt an idea or explanation. Many scientists are skeptical that Bigfoot exists.

species (SPEE-seez) A species is a group of animals or plants that share common qualities. Some researchers think Bigfoot is from a species different from humans or apes.

theories (THEE-reez) Theories are ideas that explain how or why something happens. Bigfoot researchers have theories about what kind of creature Bigfoot might be.

To Learn More

BOOKS

Teitelbaum, Michael. *Bigfoot Caught on Film: And Other Monster Sightings!* New York: Franklin Watts, 2008.

Walker, Kathryn. *Mysteries of Giant Humanlike Creatures.* New York: Crabtree, 2009.

Worth, Bonnie. *Looking for Bigfoot.* New York: Random House Children's Books, 2010.

WEB SITES

Visit our Web site for links about Bigfoot: **childsworld.com/links**

Note to Parents, Teachers, and Librarians: We routinely verify our Web links to make sure they are safe and active sites. So encourage your readers to check them out!

Index